HALLOWEEN

Pumpkin Carving Templates 201 Stencils

How To Use - Instructions

Step 1:   **Step 2**   **Step 3**

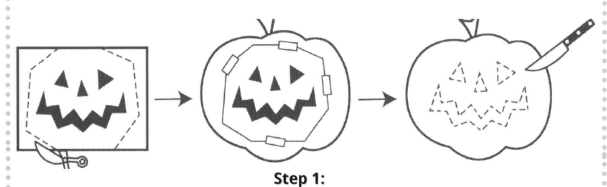

Step 1:
Cut out your chosen design.

Step 2:
Tape the design over the middle of the pumpkin. Trace the design over the pumpkin using Marker/pin/knife (to poke holes through the paper). Then connect those dots with a pen or marker, (refer back to the design if needed to ensure correct marking).

Step 3:
Lastly, using a small knife carve and cut out the design. The black areas should be fully cut out. And carve out the inside of the pumpkin.

Now place a small candle inside the pumpkin and enjoy!

Page: 114

Page: 122

GO
AWAY

Page: 128

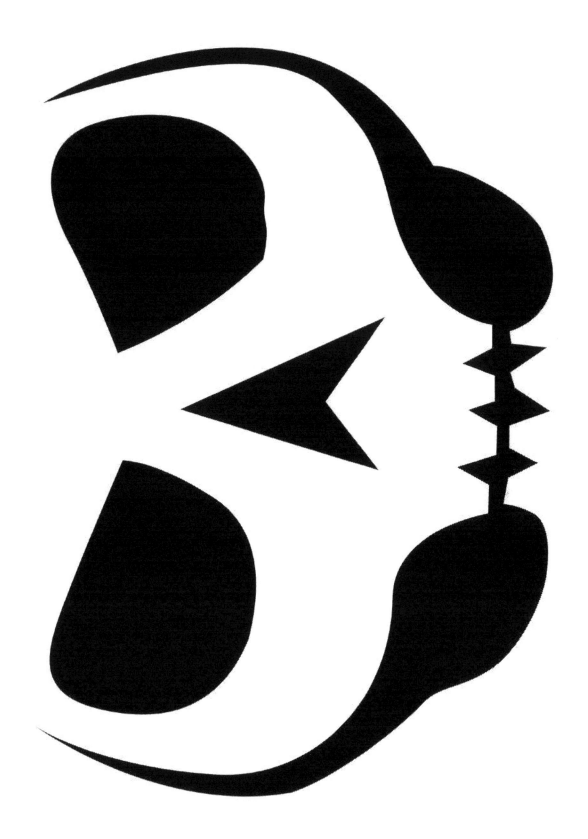

Page: 144

Page: 146

Page: 148

Page: 152

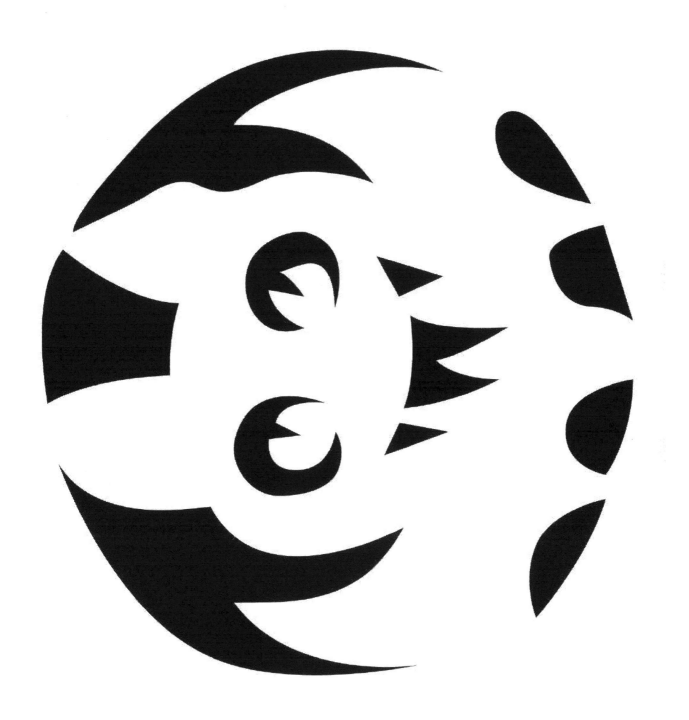

Page: 158

Page: 162

Page: 176

GO AWAY

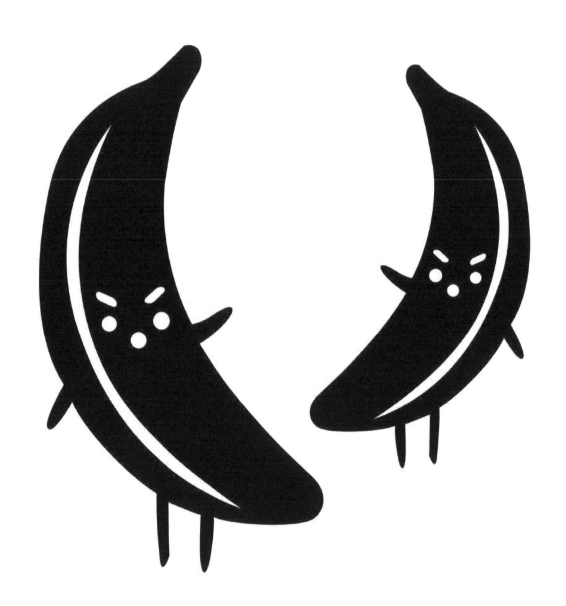

Page: 194

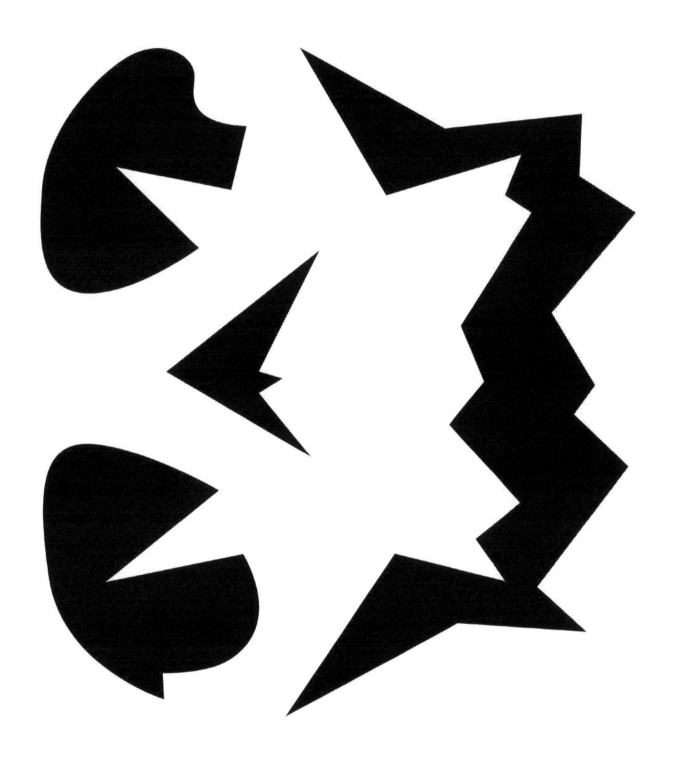

Page: 198

Page: 7

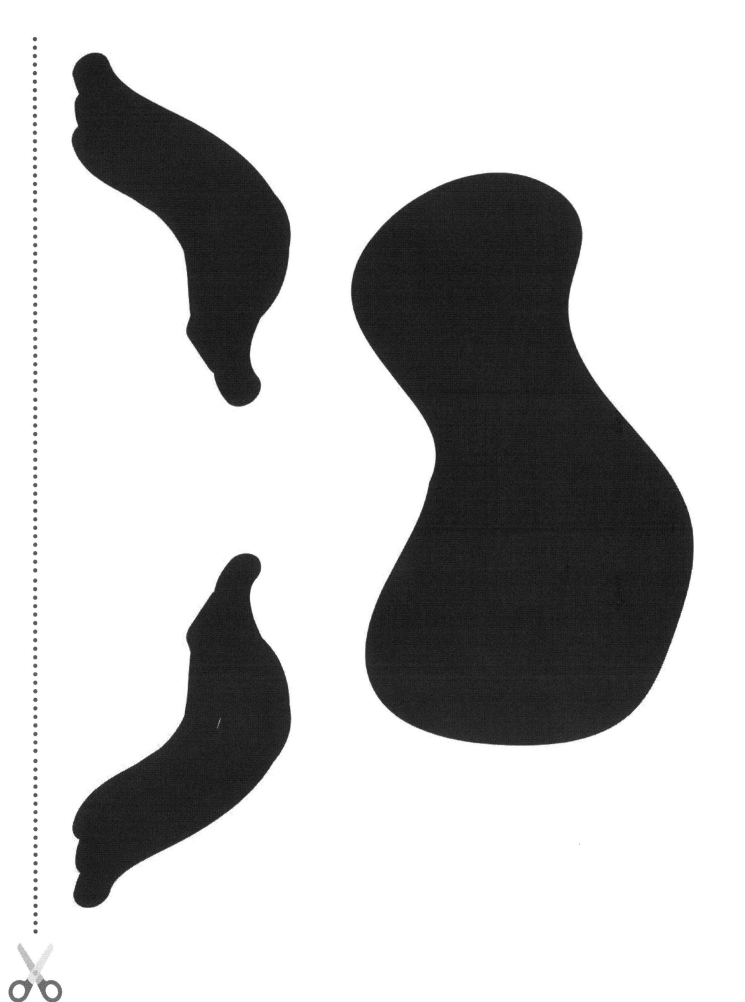

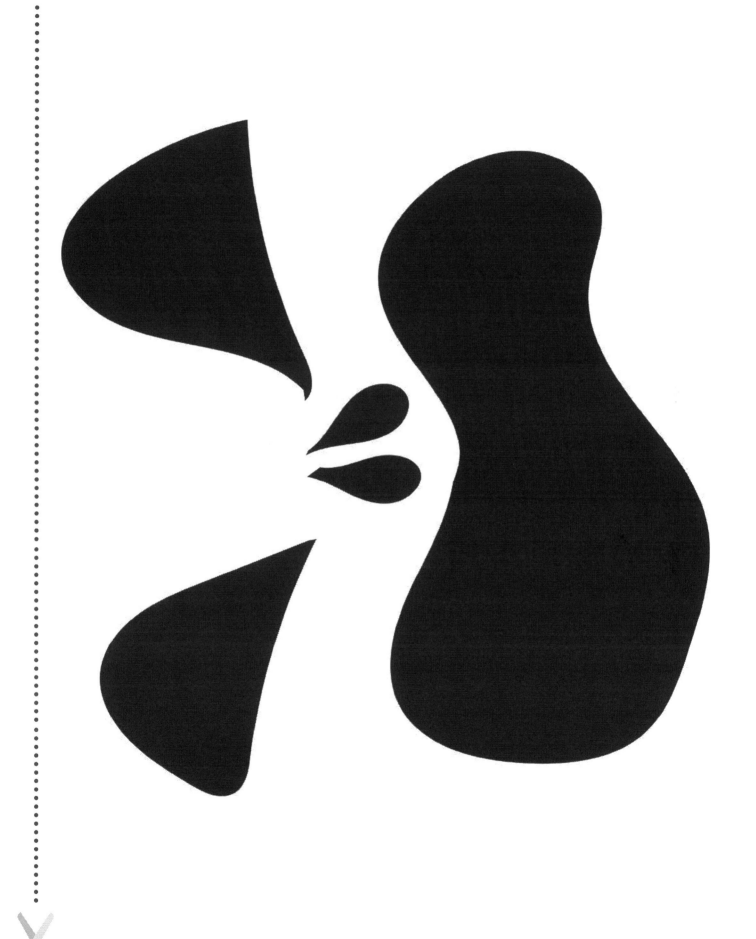

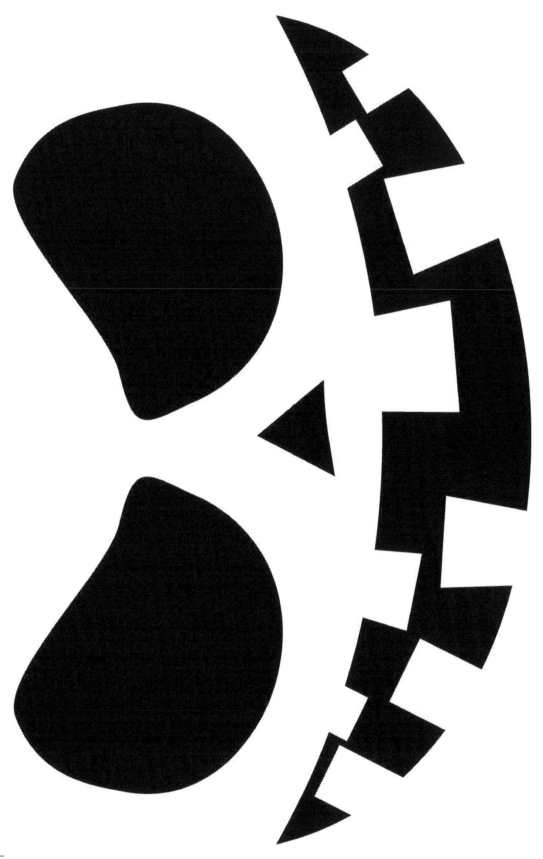

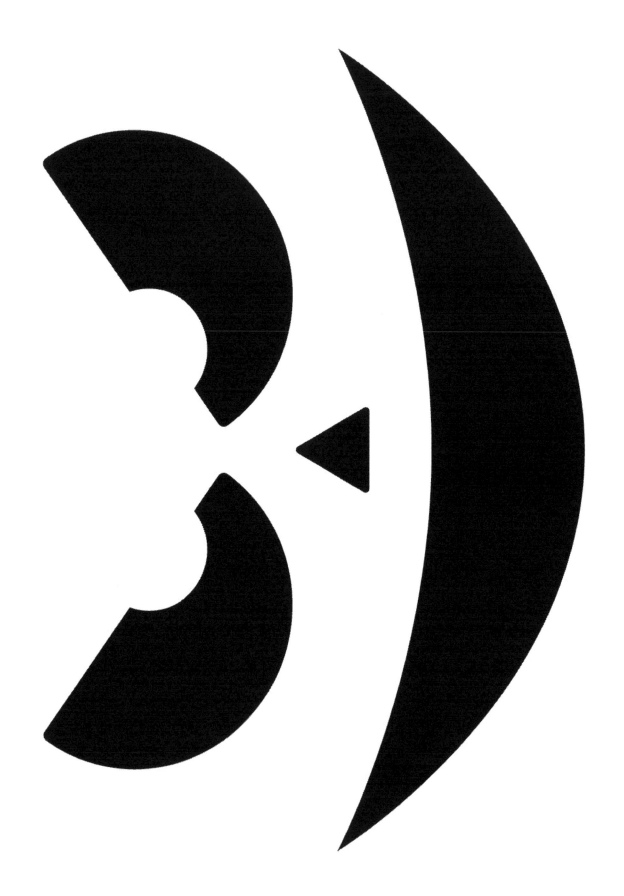

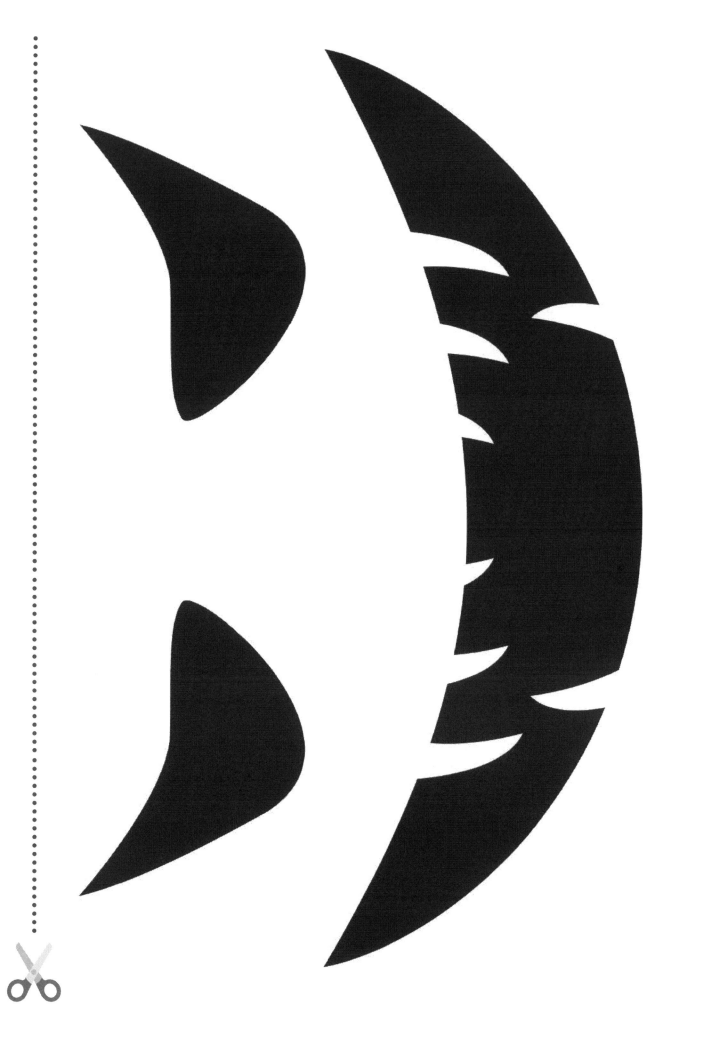

Page: 33

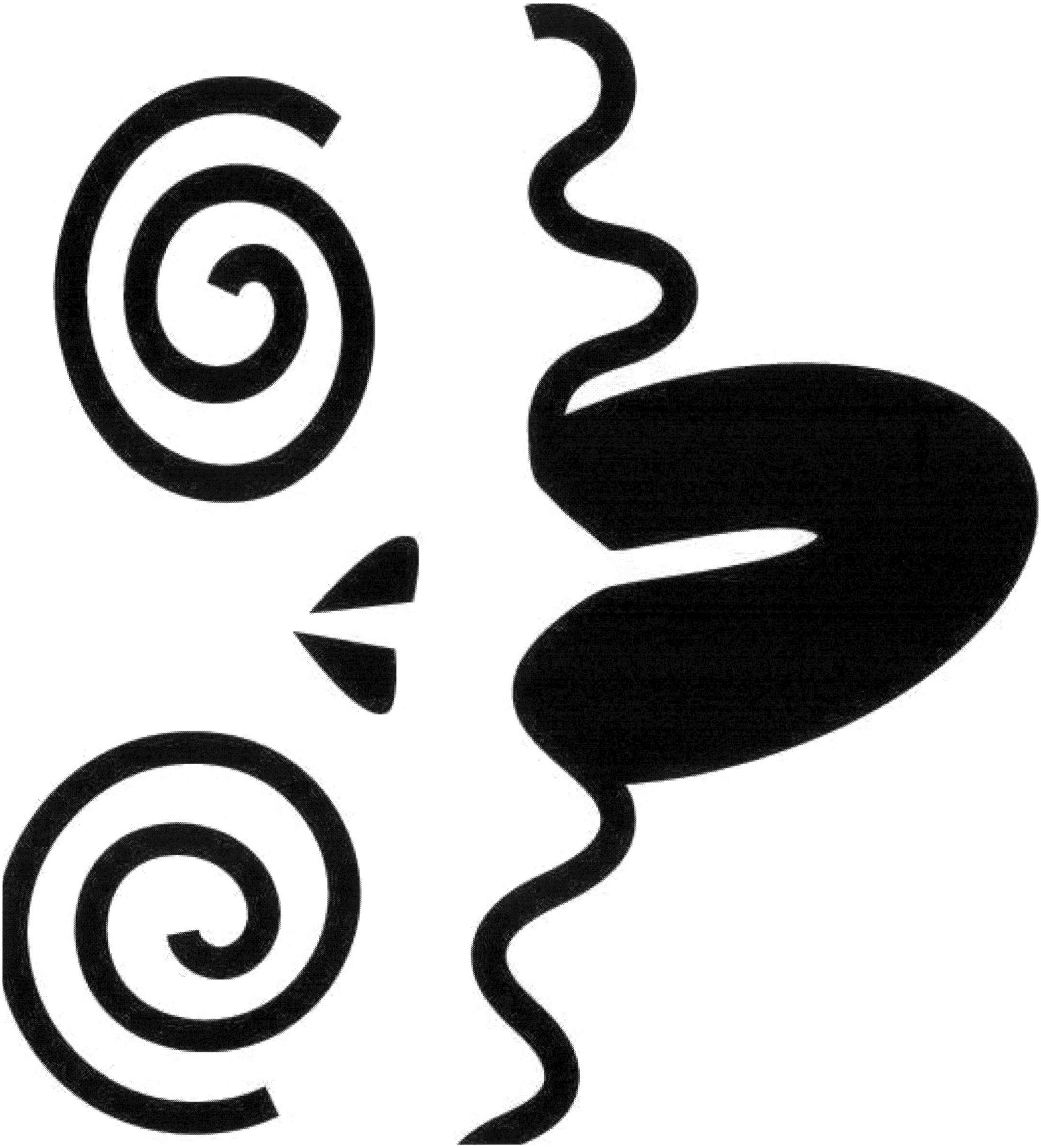

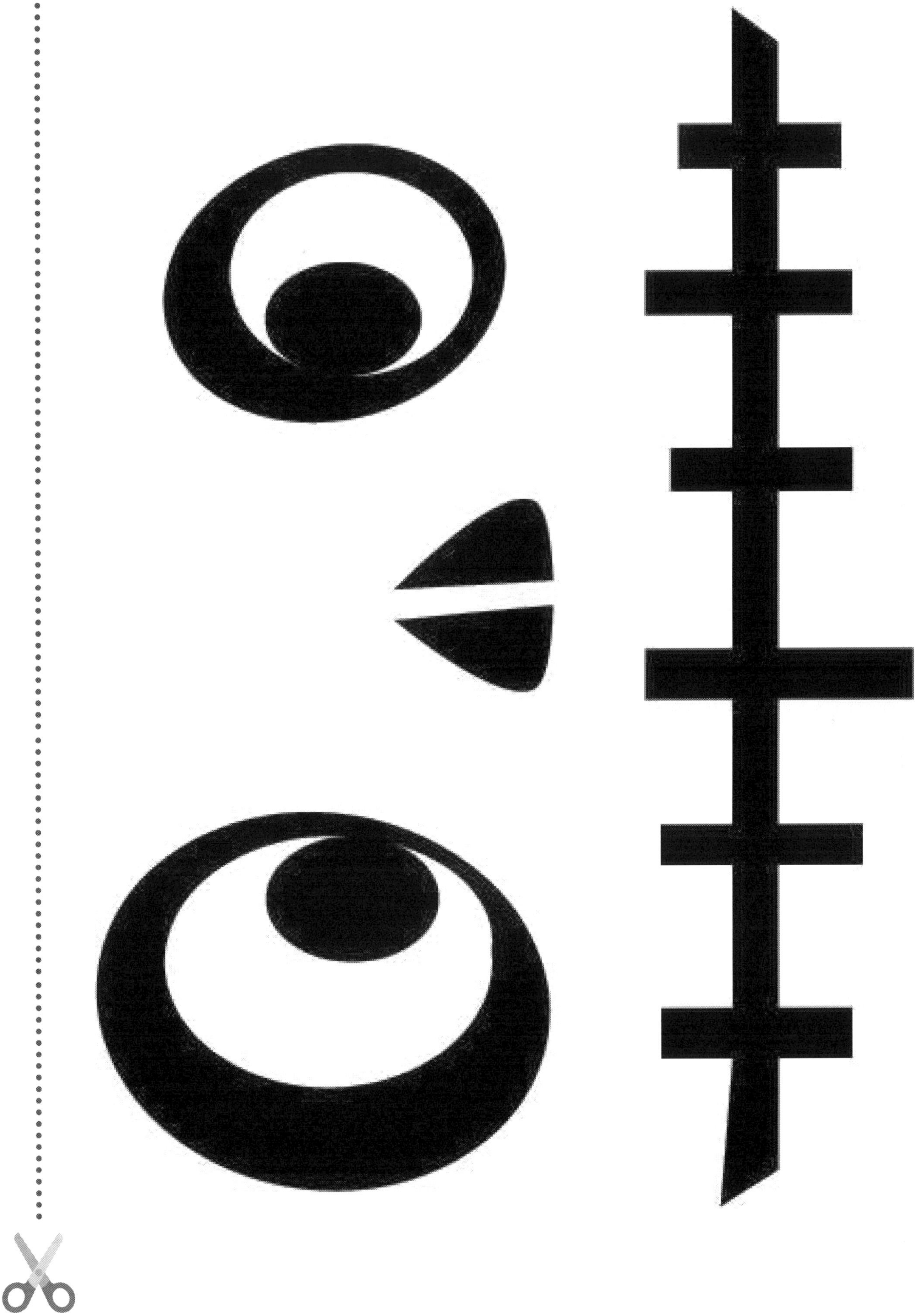

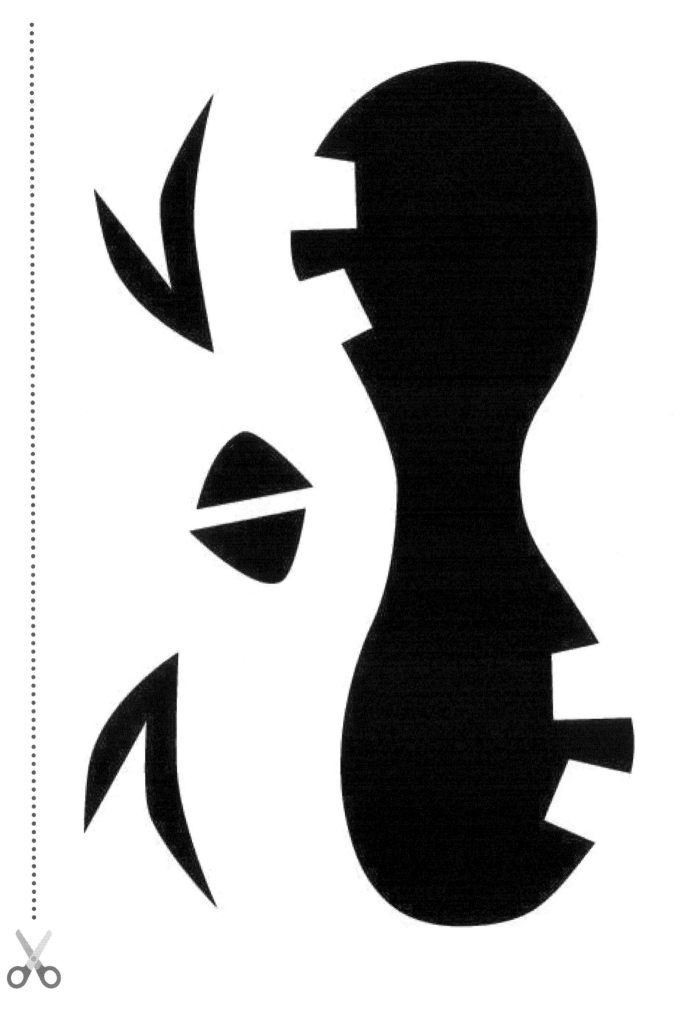

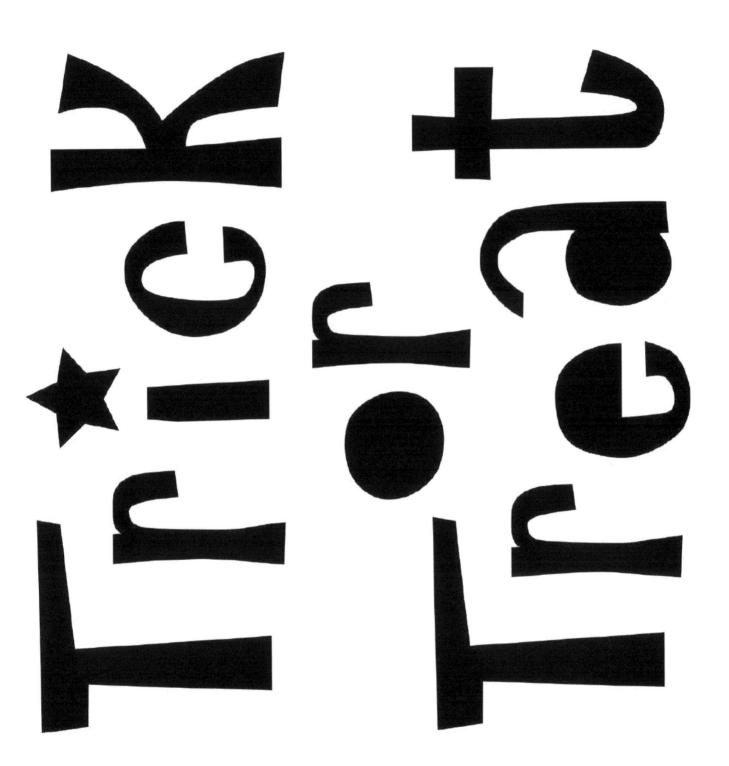

Page: 58

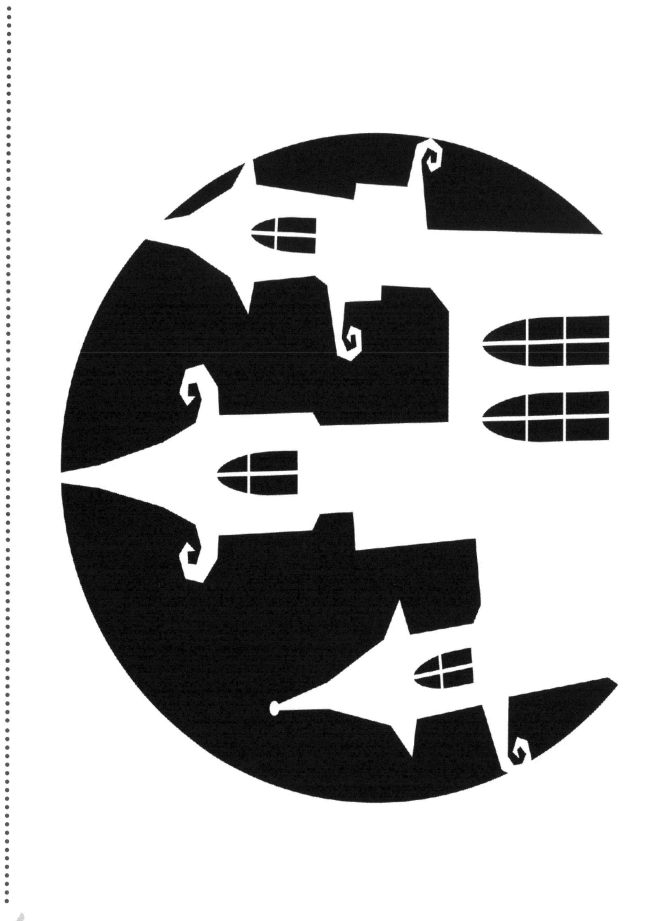

Page: 66

Page: 100

Made in the USA
Columbia, SC
13 October 2023

24433640R00111